‖‖‖ ‖ ‖‖‖‖‖‖‖‖ ‖ ‖‖‖ ‖‖‖
I0151441

★ ★ ★
LOOKING FOR NX14771

A STORY OF WAR, HEROISM AND CLOSURE

IAN HEARD

Ark House Press
PO Box 1722, Port Orchard, WA 98366 USA
PO Box 1321, Mona Vale NSW 1660 Australia
PO Box 318 334, West Harbour, Auckland 0661 New Zealand
arkhousepress.com

© Ian Heard 2019

Unless otherwise stated, all Scriptures are taken from the New Living
Translation (Holy Bible. New Living Translation copyright© 1996, 2004,
2007, 2013 by Tyndale House Foundation. Used by permission of Tyndale
House Publishers Inc., Carol Stream, Illinois 60188. All rights reserved.)

Some names and identifying details have been changed to protect the privacy
of individuals.

Cataloguing in Publication Data:
Title: Looking for NX14771
ISBN: 978-0-6488259-5-1
Subjects: History; Biography;
Other Authors/Contributors: Heard, Ian

Design by initiateagency.com

A DEDICATION

To all who've suffered loss through wars
That trampled on the hearts of those
Left to pick up pieces
And soldier on... unsung, undecorated.

IAN HEARD
March 2020

CONTENTS

★ ★ ★
CHAPTER 1
EARLIEST

I t was the first time I had ever heard a gunshot, yet I knew what it was. This little fair-headed five-year-old boy in a slovenly and unkempt backyard in Hampstead Road, Auburn, a suburb of Sydney.

I had seen the policemen through the slits between palings in the fence that stood between us and the timber-yard next door, but they had gone behind stacks of timber with the large and frenetic dog (which I now recognise as a German Shepherd), held by the neck in a rope noose at the end of a pole. They shot the dog. I didn't know its crime, but that shot and the enormity of its sound, followed by a strange, short, shuddering whine and silence stay with me even today as a seventy-six-year-old.

"Mummy, what were those policemen in the timber-yard for? Did they shoot that dog?" These were the surface questions but the deeper, unspeakable questions were those of why some things are inexplicable and full of mystery to a young mind; the mind of one whose father has not returned from the war.

Funny how some things stay with you for a lifetime. Indelible, only just sub-surface, until something—a sound, a smell, a snatch of music or a song, brings them rushing to the surface. My first experience of the primal smell of leather arrived with my little shoulder-strap school bag. I am a five-year-old schoolboy again whenever I smell fresh leather.

Sixty Hampstead Road Auburn was a run-down weatherboard, pre-war dump, but there my newly-widowed mother loved me, nurtured me and made do, as best she could for her precious son. Earliest memories are of the winter coldness and of the kerosene heater that made a valiant though inept attempt to warm us; of the doses of cod liver oil to provide needed vitamin D to keep me healthy—although I spent plenty of time outside in the sun. (The cod liver oil was an English necessity for children of less sunny climes and carried over into the Colonies). And of the leaking roof and strategically placed buckets and cans to collect drips. Then there was the shoulder-high paspalum in the backyard, always making me sticky and itchy. Who owned the house and who the landlord might be, were not matters I understood anything about. I just know that my bed had to be moved on occasions to avoid the drips—and that I was cared for tenderly and that somehow there was always food on the table.

The house next door was occupied by 'the Robeys'—one of those rogue families with undisciplined kids and any number of animals, including dogs, ferrets, chooks and the inevitable rats. Between us and them, nothing but our south-facing wall of weatherboard nailed to studs. No internal lining. So, it was not surprising was it, that one day when I was in the back room of the house, which served as bathroom, laundry and toilet, a slight sound caught my attention? I stood transfixed as a steel auger bit, maybe ½ inch diameter (yes—inches in those days), came through the timber weatherboard. And then I noticed that there were several other holes at various levels and spots around the wall…the better for the Robeys to select an appropriate one for spying! I threw some water at it and Mum later covered the holes with band-aids. We kept an eye on the wall to make sure no fresh holes appeared, but how long some of the holes had been there, I have no idea.

Maternal grandfather, William Knight lived just up the road in the family home, number 38, built by him. Six children and now (in my five-year-old eyes) an old, but generous and kindly man. He frequently walked down the hill to spend the night in the front bedroom at number 60 to provide a sense of security for Mum and me. A man of few words apart from the occasional story, and good deeds, who bequeathed childhood impressions of kindness. And generosity.

Mum's sister Rosa also lived at number 38, ALPHA, the family home up the hill.

ALPHA, capitalised in embossed copper on a painted timber board background, right there near the portentous, perhaps pretentious, front door. But then ALPHA seemed larger in memory than perhaps it really was. They said the billiard table in the sitting room was full size. A cow was said to have walked up the two steps to the secondary, side entrance to the house on one occasion, proceeded to do a lap around the billiard table and make its exit again. There was a tennis court and a paddock owned by the Knights where grandfather used to offer agistment to cattle or sheep being herded down Parramatta Road to the Flemington saleyards and abattoir. William Knight, a builder, had built the 'new' late 1930's administration buildings there at Flemington, so perhaps his connections enabled him to offer the paddock for agistment. William was also responsible for building one of the wings at Jenolan Caves House, somewhere around 1914, as well as Hurlstone, a boarding house in The Mall in Leura, and the scene of much family lore and social activity. A Trove newspaper search quickly reveals that Hurlstone, with its tennis court and lawns was a popular Leura venue for lunches and social events. Old newspapers tell us that Mrs Knight often provides a fine table for such events.

But oh, that paddock at ALPHA! What huge bonfires Mum's brothers built there for many a 'cracker night'. People walked from miles around for the spectacle of the Knight's bonfire. Lots of bonhomie and cheer and fun and laughter and adventure! The pile for the fire grew for months before Empire Day (May 24th); old car and motorcycle tyres, sump oil, discarded furniture, tree loppings and who-knows-what toxic substances found their last resting place there, all piled high around a central pole and sometimes twenty feet high! The Sydney sky was darkened for days by hundreds of these across the 'burbs. There were the legendary 'basket bombs' which, year after year, sent one of the household buckets to heaven. Where it landed no one cared; no fun police around in those days to prevent people maiming or killing themselves— or others, though reasonable steps were taken! "Basket Bomb" someone would yell, trying to be heard above the roar of the fire and fireworks and sky-rockets wizzing into the blackness to explode with glorious colour somewhere above. I never wanted it to end. The parents said trite things like, "there'll be another one next year." Next year!? They might as well have said in heaven. Kids spent the next day looking through the grass for 'unexploded ordnance'—crackers and sky-rockets somehow dropped or overlooked from someone's treasure bought with pennies scrounged and saved for months.

But Rosa had a son, my cousin Alwyn. Same age but for six weeks. We were inseparable, like twins and legends, so it seems, at mischief. But then...they moved. To the bush; well, to Branxton, which was certainly the bush in the late 1940's. Could have been another planet. I lost my nearest. And then I had to begin school and what a terror that was. Mum had to start me about three or four times because I kept walking back home. It was so big, so alien. And so inhabited by aliens. I'm sure, kind and empathetic aliens, but for this child of a war widow, still frightening. And the questions and comments from the other kids—although there had to be others in similar straits—"did your father die in the war?" "Do you only have a mother?" "Why don't you have a father?" And "hey, Tenchy doesn't have a Dad." But then there was Peggy, a gorgeous blonde, who used to take my hand at lunch time and sit with me and tell everyone we were going to get married when we grow up. Wonder what became of Peggy? At least I'm pretty sure that was her name. I do actually catch sight of her every now and again. So far as I am concerned, she still resides where she's always lived; in a shoe-box in the photo titled, Kindergarten North Auburn Public School 1948.

And then, that was all over and Tenchy embarked on the journey that took him to five primary schools and three high schools in nine years of schooling. But, before we left Hampstead Road, Tenchy became Heardy because when he was 7, his Mum married Ron Heard and suddenly he had a Dad like everyone else! But, they were going on a special holiday after the wedding and I couldn't go—and had to stay with some old aunt!

But—I had a Dad. And... he had muscles! I know because he showed them to me and I was so impressed that I told the other kids at school and they came and lined up at the front gate of 60 Hampstead Road. And I had to go and get him to come out and show them his muscles. They were impressed too; "Hey Roberts, does your Dad have muscles like that?"

"Aw, that's nothin', you should see my Dad's." And they became even more impressed because Heardy's Dad made him a great big paper kite that was the envy of every kid in the street and even the next street—and he told one envious kid that 'my Dad' would make one for him. And guess what? He did.

It was good having a Dad. But he was a trainee pastor and in those days that meant being sent to sundry and various churches for experience. That meant Auburn, Ingleburn, Merrylands, Branxton and Kurri Kurri primary schools, followed by Cessnock, Gosford and Belmont high schools. That meant 'churn' and in turn, meant that this asthmatic kid was always the new boy. It meant no long-term friends. It meant possessiveness when he did find a friend—and that usually spoiled it. But the constant had always been Mum; solid, principled, diligent and, a woman of great faith and grace and joy.

She had a small bureau with a fold-down lid that served as a desk for writing. Ink-well, pencils, paper, eraser, paper envelopes; everything was there for letter-writing or for doing homework. But the bureau also had a drawer and that drawer was filled with all manner of fascinations. Trinkets and old photographs and letters and 'special' papers that spoke of my father. And with those papers and in a large envelope, medals! Medals with beautifully coloured ribbons attached and... a dog-tag, silver plated and with a silver wrist chain and an inscription, italicised and mysteriously eductive to me:

NX 14771
E. A. TENCH. S/SGT.
B.3
C. E.
A.I.F.

And on its rear: *SYRIA*

It connected me (and does yet when I take it in my hands) in some inexplicable way, to the mysterious legend that by this time, my true father had become. For my mother had shared with me parts of the story, but it belonged to the world of the big people, the world of the grown-ups and only fragments, the fragments that fired a little boy's imagination, lodged and stayed. The imagery of soldiery; the heroism of war; the sadness of loss. And those fragments, in time, built the myth and the mystery wherein the boy's father lived—and kept on living—in his heart.

"Yes" said my mother, "one of those medals is very special; for your father did something very brave that helped a lot of people in the war." She showed me the Citation. She showed me the 'special' medal; she showed me the certificate from the Governor for his commission, but these things were too big. Once again, they belonged to the grown-up's world and understanding; they were things *they* did. But, ah yes, the war books with the Ivor Hele drawings and paintings. They were another thing altogether. In them, the war somehow became a real thing. Whenever I was at home with asthma, I would ask Mum to get them for me and I read and re-read them and gawked for hours at the drawings and paintings of the war in the Middle East and North Africa and New Guinea. Don't know what became of those books. There were three and I think one was called, **Active Service; With Australia in the Middle East** and the others I cannot remember, but there was one for each of the services, army, navy, air force. Their influence meant that whenever we were asked to draw pictures in class, mine were of spitfires and hurricanes and stick men beneath a parachute canopy—and—tanks and guns! But, increment by increment, the medals and the books and the special papers became a diminishing memory.

★ ★ ★

CHAPTER 2

ALONE-NESS AND A DOG-TAG

I liked my new father. He was provided by God and answered the prayers of my mother for a father for Ian. I remember the day I first called him Dad; it was a leap into unknown territory and yet was portentous and life-changing.

He, not a well-educated man at that time, and somewhat awkward—and certainly not given to display of affection—wrapped me in his arms in a hug. I had a father! No longer the odd-one-out. I told you about his muscles and his kite-making skills. He was also a keen vegetable gardener and soon had that paspalum-laden backyard flush with silver beet and beans, broad-beans, tomatoes and potatoes, carrots and even beetroot. That was something most tried to do in those early and austere post-war days and it meant that Ian had plenty of what makes for healthy growing and thriving. The veggies went well with and adorned (actually made edible!) the tripe and mutton and lambs-fry of those days. Mum was an excellent and imaginative cook and provider, of the standard, home style, meat-and-three-veg type. A great pastry magician, her apple pies became legendary across the family as years went by. I crave one now as I write of them.

8

Primary school was a succession of moves, as I've said. Never privy to anything that had gone before in the next new place; no history, always the newcomer, the outsider. Loneliness. And yearning. Though my new father was so good to me, there were the medals and the picture or two and the legends, hinted at by older cousins and aunts and uncles at family gatherings; little, affectionate stories of Teddy as he was called. About his happy disposition, his whistling, his photography. Photography? Yes, in civilian life, a photographer, among other skills. About how I reminded them of him, the pat on the head and the comment that my father would have been proud of me. The nostalgic voices. Mind you, they all loved Glady's new Ron and were warmly accepting and appreciative of him. He, in turn, loved them and greatly enjoyed his new family, Mum's brothers, Cecil and Cleve and sister Rosa, and their respective spouses.

Yet, in the little boy's heart, happy as he was, there remained a vague ache. How can you miss something, someone, you never knew? But he had the dog-tag. That would do. That brought him close. He took to wearing it in early teens—and tried to engrave his own name on its reverse side using the sharp point of a drawing compass, perhaps somehow to join himself with the missing owner. I can see those marks as I hold it in my hand today. Eventually the little clasp broke and Ian could no longer wear it. It was put away with the medals and... forgotten. For a while.

★ ★ ★

CHAPTER 3

A WHILE

Let me fly through the years of 'a while', the faster to carry you with me to the heart of my story.

My dear cousin Alwyn was always there. School holidays were legendary—after we recovered from the asthma with which we both suffered and was invariably brought on by the fever-pitch excitement of the weeks leading up to holidays spent together. During those lead-up weeks, letters were exchanged, great plans listed for things we'd make and places we'd go; the Clyde railway yards near Auburn, or, in Newcastle where he now lived, the harbour front wharves to watch the ships being loaded—and make nuisances of ourselves until some hand would shout, "what are you kids up to? Bugger off before I give you a good kick up the pants!".

We conned rides in steam engines at Clyde and later at Kurri Kurri in the coalfields; we built contraptions that had all the neighbourhood kids in thrall on a Saturday arvo. We near poisoned ourselves and half the neighbours with gases conjured from our chemistry sets—in the days when chemistry sets had real, worth-while chemicals in them! We frightened the daylights out of customers in his Mum's general store in

Belmont by spreading exploding (but harmless) dried crystals of nitro-gen tri-iodide on the shop floor. Punishment always ensued and we were well and truly grounded. We made bombs from gunpowder collected from fifty of the famous 'double-bunger' fire-crackers. We rode a small railway flatcar down a sloping track at an old colliery near Newcastle and de-railed it at the points. We made a flying machine that ran, sus-pended beneath the double wire clothesline, powered by positive DC voltage on one line and negative on the other—one line connecting to the electric motor via the steel wheels and the other via a wire and a brass curtain ring. We...well, never mind; the adventures went on and on. And, became, themselves, the stuff of family legend, growing with time and telling. I would visit Alwyn regularly in Newcastle as he became debili-tated with Parkinson's disease, but never lost his humour, his sense of fun and scientific and mechanical learning. Nor his deep faith and trust in God. Alwyn died as I was travelling the road to Newcastle to visit him on June 16, 2019.

Alwyn and I lived together for our last year of high school, third year, and did what was called the Intermediate Certificate, in the same class. His eldest sister, Shirley is one of the few remaining who actually remembers my father, Edward Tench. Her memories and re-telling have been of immense value. Another older cousin, Alan Knight, now with dementia, also regaled me at reunions as we grew older, with stories of my father. Precious. Alan says it was my father who got him interested in wireless, in which Alan made his career.

My new Dad also became the father of a new family member. A brother for Ian—Rodney (who much prefers Rod thank you!) whom I remember proudly wheeling around the streets and shops of Kurri Kurri in his pram. Eleven years between us, but I loved having a younger brother whose hero I could be once I was in my teens and he an impressionable little boy! I still call him 'li'l bro' and tell him if there's anything he wants to know, just to ask his big brother.

Years passed, as they seem to. My own career in business and also in Christian ministry speeding by. A wonderful wife, two outstanding boys, now in their forties, five grandchildren; one just completing her course at Sydney Design College as I'm writing this. All this and, up until the late 1990's still wondering, yet too occupied to take some time to investigate. In the early 90's, I had copies of his medals mounted on an honour board which still adorns a wall in our home, but, my biological father still remained a phantom, an enigma. Mum died before I had spent thorough or meaningful time going over these matters with her, even though the bond forged between us in those eleven years when I was her only one—her living memento of her beloved Ted—was so precious. Regret now. She seemed too sick at the end, with thyroid cancer, to get deep and meaningful with her about him and extract more information. The occupation of life and job and children and homes and....seemed to have robbed us of what we perhaps ought to have covered.

★ ★ ★

CHAPTER 4

TIME

I t was probably a year or two after Mum died.

For some reason, sitting in my office on a day that's now chiselled on memory stones, I looked up the website of the Australian War Memorial. It demonstrates, really, that the issue of identity and connection is never really far beneath the surface for any of us. It is my firm conviction that the essence of each person's ultimate identity, resides not in earthly ancestry—as rewarding a search as that can be— but in our true Source, as we shall see. Our temporal and earthly DNA is from earthly parents, but there is also within us what I like to think of as our spiritual 'DNA', sourced from the One who, we are told, had us (yes, me, you, each and every one) in mind—before time began.

I had never visited the AWM site before. It was late 1999. I was impressed with the site and, on a whim, put into the search area the initials and name of my father, E. A. Tench.

It is difficult to describe what awe-struck means, but I have experienced it. Experienced it at that moment. It was a clock-stood-still moment, now indelible. I can see it and feel it at any moment that I may choose to recall it. It is there in the never-forgotten category of memory. For there, on the screen before me with frightening imme-diacy appeared several never-before-seen photographs of my father on his motorcycle in Aley, Lebanon, together with other 7 Divison Provost men and officers with whom he served!

'Awe-struck' /ˈɔːstrʌk/ adjective: 'filled with or revealing awe' says the Oxford Dictionary. One thing to read what it means on a page in the dictionary; another to experience, as I did at that moment. I froze, unable to look away, hoping the 'phone wouldn't ring; somehow afraid that the images might disappear or fade away, or worse, that it was my imagina-tion. Time passed as I considered and stared. Be careful, you might lose them! I saved them to desktop and ordered some printed copies online. For the next several days I revisited the site and put his initials and name in again, making sure. I showed my wife, my sons, cousins, friends, anyone who'd listen—or even not listen! Something had happened; a process of connection had begun; curiosity was suddenly insatiable. He *was* real! There he was in Aley, Lebanon with another Provost, Warrant Officer I F E Harris together with their CO, Captain John Grimshaw proudly astride their Norton Model 16H single-cylinder 500 cc. motor-cycles. The pictures were dated 24th August 1941.

But, so much more lay ahead....

★ ★ ★

CHAPTER 5

BOMANA

A tropical Spring-morning sun bore down through a thin membrane of cirrus cloud above, encouraging birdsong, and filtering fitfully through the lush foliage of the Rain Trees that bordered and defined the wide cemetery. Beneath these trees was dense shade except for small bright patches where the sunlight won its way through, revealing the verdant nap of well-cared for lawn. In contrast, the wide un-shaded hectares away from the trees were punctuated every two metres by 3779[1] marble headstones standing to attention, a ghost-army, in military-precision formation.

It was October 5, 2002 and three men stood at the top of the gentle slope that accommodates this infamy, grappling with what all that marble meant. For at once it represented so much— salvation for many Australians from what-might-have-been; death nonetheless to these thousands; heroism, yet death nonetheless; a measure of dignity, yet death nonetheless. Overwhelmingly, it represented curtailed possibilities. For it was, and is, a field full of the cruelly never-to-be-realised

---

[1] The number in 2002. At the time of writing in 2019, it is above 3820 as more have been located and identified.

dreams and hopes of all those 18, 19 and 20-something year old men—and one woman.

The whole gently sloping hillside was itself also a slight depression, as though the very earth itself had sagged under the enormous weight of the oceans of grief and loss represented there.

The three men also sensed the weight as they walked in the reverence it demanded, down the hillside, past and through row upon silent row of frozen memory and potential.

The sun that day, warmed grave number B1.F.15 just as it had, more than twenty-one thousand times since its occupant was laid there. His age, recorded on the headstone, 30 years, was among the oldest of all the dead. The name engraved there is that of Lieutenant Edward Alfred Tench MM. In engraved, Formal Roman capitals, the epitaph reads, in words from Thomas Campbell's poem, 'Hallowed Ground',

TO LIVE IN HEARTS
WE LEAVE BEHIND
IS NOT TO DIE

There the three men came to an almost awkward standstill, read the words and embraced. For the moment, words would have seemed vulgar and intrusive. Eventually they made soft comments and placed their floral tribute and took photographs and tried to think of appropriate responses. They lingered in the warmth of sun and moment; lingered as though perhaps expecting something further to impinge on their senses; a sight, a sound, a sudden mysterious zephyr. There was nothing except the stillness, the distant birdsong and the inescapable immanence of all those headstones and what they represented. And of one headstone, and what it represented, to them.

Yet there *was* something; and there *was* a voice. First, within, a sigh and a sense of mission accomplished, of overdue respect now shown. Then, the 'voice' of silent lament, rising up from the very deepest part of self-awareness. The awesome realisation of a kind of substitution—of their being here because he, Edward Tench—and all these—were not...

Of the first martyr, Abel, it is recorded that God lamented, 'his blood cries out to me from the ground.' The same cry is, as it were, heard here also. It speaks too; of injustice and agony and separation from all that might have been; but also, so articulately, of cause and courage and cost—and of folly and waste and grief. It's a lament over the sad necessity for people to defend from invaders, their lands and homes and children and peaceful existence.

The lingering of the three, myself and my two dear sons, was also to extract the most from this brief and poignant moment of culmination. Compared with the passing of those twenty-one thousand suns, this moment seemed but an unregistrable flicker, but there we stood, hearing, feeling, sensing what the place spoke.

The post-nominal letters MM stand for Military Medal, the equivalent of the Military Cross for non-commissioned ranks. It was instituted by King George V in 1916 to correspond with the Military Cross for non-commissioned ranks for acts of gallantry and devotion to duty under fire. Of the 993,000 Australian men and women to go to World War 2, just over 1000 were awarded the Military Medal.

This was not my first visit, nor would it be my last. I had actually viewed the grave once before—but for a moment in 1980, during a business trip to Port Moresby and New Guinea when my sons were pre-teens. Now was the time to bring them here and pay proper respect. Besides, I had begun the process of piecing together my father's story and wanted my boys involved. What a shame I had not done more of this before my mother's death in 1993.

Edward Tench, a photographer in civilian life, had married my mother on Saturday 31st October, 1936. By 1940, having been married four years with no children, Edward enlisted at Paddington on May 13 as a volunteer for the new Division being raised for the war effort. He was initially allocated to 7 Division Engineers, but his papers show that he was moved almost immediately to the newly raised 7 Division Provost Corps. Provost being the now 'sanitised' name for Military Police because none would volunteer for the post that had, sadly, earned a somewhat sullied reputation in World War 1.

Nevertheless, here we were, at the Bomana War Cemetery, blessed with a beautiful day. We had been driven there from our hotel in Port Moresby by Daniel, the driver for the CEO of a large engineering contractor in Moresby. Because I was a member of the Royal Prince Alfred Yacht Club in Sydney, I had contacted the Royal Papua Yacht Club in the hope of perhaps having a sail whilst there. I informed them of my purpose in Moresby and, to my surprise was contacted by the club President who offered to take us under his wing and look after us. And he did, right royally—taking us out off the coast fishing and facilitating things for us, including very kindly providing car and driver to take us to Bomana and out to McDonald's Corner on the way to the start of the infamous Track. Unfortunately, the road from McDonald's Corner out to Ower's Corner at that time was not negotiable in the sedan we were in, so we didn't get to see the true start of the track.

The next day we bravely hired ourselves a car. We felt there was more to be done and, at the suggestion of eldest son Adrian we again visited the cemetery and made a charcoal rubbing of that beautiful headstone. We then paid our respects at the grave of Bruce Kingsbury VC, nearby, before driving on to find and photograph the site of the field Hospital where Edward Alfred Tench died on January 12, 1943. The 2/9 Australian General Hospital had been a sprawling tent city under the brow of Hombrom's Bluff, about 17 miles (27 Km) from Port Moresby.

★ ★ ★

CHAPTER 6

THE MILITARY MEDAL AND THE
MEN WHO SAVED AUSTRALIA

I n the days when Australia was still being reluctantly weaned by Mother England, her wars were our wars, her awards and military decorations became ours. Their Distinguished Conduct Medal followed the VC as the second honour for gallantry or bravery in the field. The award of the DCM also carried pay and pension emoluments for the recipient and so, according to historian Frank Richards—

"There were no grants or allowances with the Military Medal, which without a shadow of a doubt had been introduced to save awarding too many DCMs. With the DCM went a money-grant of twenty pounds, and a man in receipt of a life pension."[2]

So, the Military Medal and the Distinguished Conduct Medal can be considered pretty much equivalent awards for bravery in the field. A description of the Military Medal appears in the Appendix of this book.

But, to return to my train: as already stated, just under one million Australian personnel served in the Second World War. Of that million,

---

[2] Richards, Frank. 'Old Soldiers Never Die' (Library of Wales) (Kindle Locations 1742-1745). Parthian Books. Kindle Edition. Quoted from Wikipedia.

about 1000 were recipients of The Military Medal for bravery in the field. E. A. Tench was one of them. The Citation for the award is also included in the Appendix.

For many years that Citation, along with some other important papers had sat in a bureau drawer. The dog-tag was given more prominence as it seemed to connect me more with him. After all, it bore his name and number, incidentally a number that had been inerasably printed in my sub-conscious since earliest memory. NX14771 seems like a line from a poem recited for a school play or exam and which cannot, will not, be shaken from the mind despite years and troubles and travels and thousands of other important matters. Following hard on my on-line encounter with my father, I now began to look with fresh eyes and to see the import of that Citation and accompanying papers and to examine their context.

As my research intensified, I one day came across the transcript of an ABC 4Corners programme from 1998. As I read it, I was transfixed by the enormity of what had been accomplished in New Guinea just to the north of Australia, first by our Militia, who should not even have been there, and then by our 7th Division men. One of those interviewed was Professor David Horner of our Australian National University in Canberra. His knowledge impressed me. On impulse I hurried off an email to 'Aunty' ABC, 'I have just read a transcript of your 4Corners programme of April 27, 1998, *The men who saved Australia* and would like to acquire a copy of the videotape. Is it available at the ABC shops? My father was 7 Div in the Middle East and Greece, where he was awarded The Military Medal for bravery—and then on Kokoda where he died.'

To my surprise my answer came within half an hour, 'Mr Heard, we're dubbing a copy for you right now. Please provide your address and we'll mail it straight to you—no charge'! I was moved and most appreciative.

The programme was a masterful account by Chris Masters of what occurred on the inglorious Kokoda Track. It featured some of Damien Parer's award winning footage of those 'ragged bloody heroes' labouring up that heavy, mud-layered track. 4Corners had found some of them, now aged, yet nevertheless recognisable from Parer's films, and had sat with them to talk it through. They were old heroes, every one of them. Heroes then in black and white but in the here and now, in colour, as though at last being afforded the dignity that the reality of colour seemed to bring. Beings, at last, of this world—the now world; not just of a long-forgotten world when men and deeds and actions were monochrome.

It is an extraordinarily moving account as Jack Manol, Lindsay Bear, Jim Moir, Jack Sim, Keith Norrish and others re-live the ghastly conditions, the deprivation, not to mention the ignorance that pitted ill-equipped men against the imperial might of Japan. Our 39th Battalion Militia men fought and defended with inadequate food, inadequate medical supplies and woefully inadequate training or equipment, to hold off the Japs against all odds. Four hundred and fifty against thousands of Japanese (some 14,000 were landed)! These valiant men held back the tide until the arrival of the 7th Division men—healthy, trained, bronzed and fit, "they looked like gods to us," said Jack Manol.

'Teddy' Edward Tench was one of them. And he died there, not of bullets, shrapnel or shells; no, it was scrub typhus that claimed his life as it did so many—as did malaria too. He was with General Blamey; he was with the mythic Ralph Honner; he was all the way across the Track maintaining lines of communication, guarding Japanese POW's, keeping discipline and helping ensure that reliability of supplies and evacuation of wounded went as smoothly as the trying conditions allowed. It was late 1942.

But we must go back, prior to Kokoda and New Guinea, for the real story of my father's heroism occurred in Greece. Yes, Greece, and to Greece we will go in just a little while. After I tell you about the Diaries! Oh...and the book; and the colleagues! Patience, reader!

★ ★ ★

CHAPTER 7

THE DIARIES!

I mentioned that I was impressed by Professor David Horner of ANU, interviewed in 'The men who saved Australia.' Impressed enough and emboldened enough to approach him for assistance. I found an email address on the ANU website and, with a nothing ventured, nothing gained spirit, I contacted him—uncertain whether he would respond to unsolicited email; or, if he did, when a response might come.

'Dear Professor Horner: I saw you interviewed in the 1998 4Corners programme, 'The men who saved Australia' with Chris Masters. My father, Edward Tench NX14771 was 7 Div. Provost and after the Middle East and Greece, was on Kokoda. He died in New Guinea of scrub typhus. He had been awarded the Military Medal for bravery in Greece. Are you able to assist me in my research of him and where might I find information about him and 7 Div. Provost?'

'Dear Ian' came the response, perhaps 40 minutes later! It went something like this; 'thank you for your email. May I suggest that you visit the Australian War Memorial in Canberra. Before you visit, make contact and arrange a time and ask them to have ready the appropriate War

Diaries of 7 Div Provost for Middle East, Greece and New Guinea. But I also recommend that you read a book titled, 'The Other Enemy, Australian Soldiers and the Military Police' by Glenn Wahlert. I do hope these suggestions are helpful in your search for information about your father.

Kind regards,

David Horner.'

I had no idea that such Diaries were available to view. My ignorance! So, a trip to Canberra was duly planned. This was before the Diaries had been digitised and made available online, a current and ongoing AWM project.

Now, unless you have experienced the uncanny chill of opening files containing old pages with both typewritten and handwritten notes on them, it is difficult to convey the mingled senses of querulous antic-ipation, impatience, and the excitement of discovery. And yes, what discovery there was. For those old pages contained thrill after thrill. Sometimes on a day to day basis—my father was there. He was there! We had entered but a few pages into that historic realm when the name Tench began to appear to my younger son, Gavin, on one side of the table with the New Guinea Diaries and my wife and I on the other side, with the North Africa and Middle East Diaries. Details were there, of events and conditions, from the mundane to the glorious; but even the glorious flattened out and somehow rendered mundane by the officialese of Captain Grimshaw or others whose task it was to daily write up the orders and the events of the day. For example, from Greece, handwritten with neat penmanship:

'Lamia April 17

Fine. All Co's en Convoy from Pharsalos to Thebes. Volume of traffic increasing in density. O. C's of convoys advised to increase speed. Roads bombed and machine gunned continuously. Members performed their duty under trying circumstances.

Severe blockage of traffic on North Pass near Lamia due to enemy severely bombing and machine gunning the roads. Ammunition truck set on fire and with the assistance of Corporal Pearce ammunition removed. Lamia received a severe bombing attack at 1415 hours. Also Straight Road from Lamia to Bralos Pass… Exceptionally fine work was performed by Sgt Harris, L/Cpls Swinfield and Hunt. Camp site bombed and machine gunned, decided to move camp to a position near foot of Bralos Pass…

April 18

Town (Lamia) burning fiercely 0715 hrs Cnl Rodgers 1 Aust Corps, visited bivouac seeking information as to whether the 21st Bn NZ forces had retired along the Volos road to Molos.

Informed the Cnl regarding Cpl Pearce's patrol in the early hours of that morning and there had been no contact with NZ or any other troops on that road.

Informed Cnl Rodgers that I would send a Don. R to seek the required information from NZ BHQ Molos, Cnl Rodgers concurred and requested that such intelligence be sent to Bgdr Lee, commander of Lee Force, Domokos. Received despatch from Cnl Rodgers for Bgdr Lee.

*Sgt **Tench**, Cpl Pearce left at 0730 hrs for Molos, BHQ,
with instructions to proceed to Bgdr Lee, Domokos. Sgt Tench
and Cpl Pearce returned at 1530 hrs their task completed.'*

As it turns out, those two days, April 17 and 18 of 1941 were cru-
cial days in the evacuation of the Allied Forces (including Australia's
6th Division) from Greece under the relentless and withering advance
of the German war machine. The activity of April 18 in which Edward
Tench and, it appears, Corporal Pearce, were involved is here set down
in a few lines. The Citation provides more detail but it is not known
whether Corporal Pearce accompanied Teddy all the way to Domokos
or if his part in the mission was completed at Molos at the NZ Brigade
Headquarters. In any case Edward Tench was the senior rank in charge
of the mission.

Excitedly we put markers in pages to be copied and received con-
structive and willing assistance from the AWM staff. I began to feel
connected; across 60 years, I was touching my father. He was taking
shape. Becoming real, an actual person who did things both ordinary
and glorious and whose deeds—at least some of them—were recorded
as though for me. My father was emerging before my eyes; the myth,
materialising; the phantom, taking flesh!

Humour was there too, albeit clothed in the same officialese; like
police-speak. As when a contingent of Provost was sent to investigate
why dynamite seemed to be missing from stores inventory. Yes, of course!
What else might Australian country boys do with dynamite, but go fishing? No better, quicker way to get a load of fresh fish than a stick of
dynamite in the river to stun or kill them and have them all float to the
surface for hand-harvesting! Or, what about the truck commandeered

for official purposes only to be found running cases of beer and grog from Beirut to the camps. Resourceful these Aussies—especially when it comes to grog. Worth a day or two in the lockup!

For the son of Edward Tench, sitting before those storied pages, the diaries contained many lump-in-the-throat moments. Perhaps none more than the entry in which Captain Grimshaw (himself a recipient of the Military Cross) praised, again in constrained language, those Provost who had stood with him to see the very last evacuees through to Athens and nearby coastal beaches where ships stood off to receive them. The motto of the Provost in World War II was, 'First in: Last out.' It described very well the duties involved in being among the first up to help establish the front to facilitate communication lines, logistics, access for traffic and equipment including guns, trucks and ambulances. True to their motto, Grimshaw's entry on April 23 1941, reads—

Thebes 23 April 1941

*'Fine and windy. Patrols and Point Duty men posted. Delayed action and HE[3] bombs dropped on Thebes Railway Station. Took over complete traffic control from CMP at 2300 hrs. RSM and remainder of Coy not detailed for duty, sent to evacuation point, "D" beach. CAPT Grimshaw, SGT Harris, **CPL Tench**, Delaney, George, SGT Maddern, CPL Pearce, Batenby, LCLs Potts and McEvoy, Mallyon and Barnes. **These are the men who remained on duty in and around Thebes, until all troops and convoys had been***

---

[3] Physical description: a German Second World War 50kg HE bombs, designed for general demolition. It is 110cm long, 20.3cm diameter (body), and had an explosive charge of approximately 23kg. (From Imperial War Museum website)

safely conducted through the town. Delayed action bombs exploding through the night. The party left at 1230 hrs for evacuation point, "D" beach.'

"D" Beach was at Porto Rafti, in Attica, east of Athens on the Aegean Sea, today a beautiful tourist stopover with an innocence that denies that anything so dark and terrible could have occurred there. Injured, battle-fatigued, chilled-to-the-bone, desperate men, now under that fatalistic and final order; 'every man for himself.'

They were all heroes, medals or none; and the Greeks saw them as such. Saw them as rescuers …liberators; and have never forgotten what the Australians and New Zealanders did. Here are some paragraphs from the pages of a hand-written personal diary of one of the 7 Div Provost Coy about whom I'll tell you shortly. I introduce these diary notes now because they so well describe the awful conditions.

You will recall some of the Provost duties outlined previously and understand that in the evacuation, they were responsible for the smooth movement southward of thousands of trucks, armoured vehicles, troops and Greek civilians through the often-mountainous terrain of Greece and in winter conditions with frequent freezing snow.

'Firstly, before I start, I will give you an idea of the work we were engaged in. It consisted mainly of convoy duty over the mountains, which called for hard and skilled riding[4] and many long hours on the job. Sometimes one grew tired of it all, but then that was the job so we kept on day after day

---

4   On motorcycles

seeing the boys up to the front, then up we went and things got very warm from then on-wards....

All troops evacuated their positions from Ellison (?) fighting a hard rear-guard action all the way but still the Hun comes on, but many thousands fall foul to the ANZAC's fire.

All troops are slowly but surely retreating to the 3rd line of defence at Bralos Pass 7 miles Sth of Lamia. This move-ment was carried out mainly at night which called for a lot of skill and nerve to take these men back further to escape the hell of fire, blood and snow which these men had endured for the last 2 weeks. But alas it was of no avail as you will read further on. Our camp, 3 miles Nth of Lamia is sighted by the Hun and then he gave us hell, machine gunning and bomb-ing us but we were lucky and only sustained one casualty....

Later—

'This day I shall always remember for he literally blasted Lamia from under our feet. We had escapes too remarkable and numerous to mention so after the troops had retired through the town it was time for us to go. (Note to reader: 'first in, last out')

My bike had been blown up so I jumped aboard the cob-ber's and away we went......

As we rode up over the mountains I turned and saw bomb-wracked Lamia, deserted and burnt to the ground...[5]

---

[5] From handwritten diary of Norman McFarland

Ah…but the Diaries held another surprise, for they reveal that after action in the Middle East and, for Edward Tench and some others, Greece—the Australian 7th Division was brought home briefly for preparation and deployment in the Pacific theatre. And that is how I came to be here! Mind you, it was but a few days 'home leave' in August 1942, but it was enough time for Edward and Gladys to perform the necessary duty that brought Ian into this world! But a few days, after some six years of marriage, and, after which Edward embarked from Brisbane on August 10, 1942, never to return.

We are, each and every one, here on purpose; but it can truly be said, I just squeaked in!

★ ★ ★

CHAPTER 8

THE OTHER ENEMY!

P rofessor David Horner, you'll remember, had recommended a book, 'The Other Enemy' with the sub-title, 'Australian Soldiers and the Military Police', by Glenn Wahlert.

Flush with our success with the Diaries at the Australian War Memorial, we were now hot on E A Tench's trail. That trail was not nearly as cold as we thought it might be, and—we had a certain sense of a special Superintendence over our search! I hope that you, like me, may see this too, as the story unfolds.

One of my sons, Gavin, with me, decided to visit the State Library in Sydney to view microfiche files of old newspapers. We knew that there was a story somewhere about Teddy's bravery and the award of The Military Medal. We had also determined to view a copy of Glenn Wahlert's book whilst there, so, after finding and copying the newspaper article from The Cumberland Argus (if you please!) of January 14, 1942, we asked to see a copy of the book.

This turned out to be another of 'those' moments! As we stood with the book in our hands, I turned to the index at the rear to look for Seventh Division, but before I found those words, Gavin stabbed his finger into the page, saying, "there he is, 'Tench, Staff Sergeant Edward…. Page 111'"! and fingers tripped over thumbs as I found every page but 111! And then, there indeed he was, in an abbreviated excerpt based on the Citation for The Military Medal, '*Staff Sergeant Edward Tench's motorcycle was continuously bombed and machine gunned. His action assisted the successful withdrawal of Lee Force, for which he received an M.M.*' And, on another page, one of the photographs I had found on the day I first went to the AWM website! Why? Because author Glenn Wahlert's purpose was to show how the somewhat sullied reputation of Military Police from WW1 had been well and truly redeemed by the Provost of WW2. Of course, even their name had been somewhat sanitised. 'Provost' did not carry the unsavoury taste that Military Police, rightly or wrongly had engendered in soldiers' minds. "Provost', arising as it did from the worlds of academia and jurisprudence, had a more 'up-market' ring to it! Whether this successfully prevented them being aka 'the other enemy' is perhaps debatable, given Australians' dislike of authority or anything that might stand between them and a good time! It does seem, by and large, that their own attitudes and deeds in the WW2 theatre, largely won respect and admiration. Mind you, there were of course plenty of heroes among them in the first war too, but generally, deserved or not, they had been seen as layabouts who were pretty much a waste of space, food and oxygen who spoiled everybody's fun! Their duties in both wars (and I'm sure more recent conflicts) do include limiting alcohol consumption and visits to brothels and general skylarking that Aussies are so prone to engage in. It is worth noting that Provosts/MP's have quite far-ranging authority including authority to place any soldier (including the highest ranks) under arrest for drunk and disorderly behaviour, affray, desertion and sundry other offences.

So, to return to Glenn Wahlert's treatise. Not only had he searched out those among the Provost who had distinguished themselves, but he is also quite effusive in his praise of their general discipline and their effectiveness and the indispensable contribution made, especially in situations like that in Greece and Crete.

The Ambulance Corps could not speak highly enough of the actions of the Provosts in Greece as a quote from Matt Walsh's 'The Battle for Greece and Crete' reveals; *'On the 18th April the men of the 2/1ˢᵗ Field Ambulance were bringing back wounded from Larissa and had this to say about the Provosts. - 'we got through the roads with the wounded, due to the fine work being done at great personal risk by the Provost; without their tireless efficiency many men and vehicles could not have reached safety.'*

★ ★ ★
CHAPTER 9
"...WHO'S CALLING?"

"I'm sorry, my father died a few months ago." I knew the voice was too young to be that of the man with whom I had hoped to speak. My heart sank as I apologised.

Yes, I had been in touch with author Glenn Wahlert: did he know of any 7 Div Provost who might be still alive? His book had been published in 1999 and his research done over several years prior to that. And, it was now somewhere around the end of 2003. Was this to be the end of the trail? All dead? all gone? no opportunity? Oh well, let's try the next name on the list of three or four given me by Glenn.

Tentatively and with some trepidation I dialled the next number. He lived at Asquith, a Sydney suburb perhaps 20 kilometres from my home. An older voice answered.

"Is this Norman McFarland?" I asked gingerly. I say gingerly because, you must realise, I could not know what I might be uncovering. What disappointment might meet me—like, "That Tench scoundrel! Still owes me twenty quid. He was a real piece of work." Of course, these possibilities had wriggled into my consciousness. Did I really want to do this? After all, I didn't know him and there might be others who did!

"Yes" said the smart, elderly voice.
"Were you Seventh Division Provost in World War Two?"
His, "Yes sir!" sounded military enough for my pulse to quicken and my sweat glands to announce they were in perfect working order.
"Does the name Edward, or Teddy Tench mean anything to you?" I squeaked out in a voice that didn't sound at all like mine. There; it was out. Now—wait for the crash and burn—or ....

"Teddy!" in startled exclamation. For a moment I think he thought I was Teddy... "Oh my word—Teddy!" he repeated... "A wonderful fellow. Remember? Couldn't forget a chap like that. We were together in the show in the Middle East and then they took some of us over to Greece for the evacuation...oh boy what a business that was; didn't think any of us'd get out of that. I was at Bralos Pass with Teddy when the Hun came galloping down on us—tanks, troops, field guns, stookas overhead, it got very hairy; he got a gong for bravery, you know. Rode his machine down to Volos and then up to Domokos; roads all bombed and under fire. Another time he was there when I had my bike blown up almost from under me..." And Norman went on. And on, with tales of Teddy and others until, perhaps 3 or 4 minutes later he paused ...

"Who's calling?" he asked; to a choked-up-with-relief, joy, surprise, pride and gratitude all rolled-into-one massive EMOTE—Ian!

I found it hard to sound the words. I had to summon all my self-discipline to remain calm as I said, "well, my name is Ian—and I am Teddy's son."

Silence. Then, "you're Teddy's son!? Where are you? Is Ted still with us? There's not many of us left. Tell me about yourself. How did you find me?" The questions came like a torrent. He remembered being interviewed for the book, retelling stories to Glenn Wahlert. But, and most important of all, he remembered those events of sixty-going-on-seventy years ago, as though they had occurred last week! What is it about going through grave and critical circumstances with others, that leaves an indelible—yes, and not just indelible—but an almost ever-present, chiselled-in-stone impression, within? These events were so large, so all-consuming, surreal and defining, that nothing in life thereafter is capable of surmounting or erasing them. Not surprising that men and women who have been through such trial find real life so difficult to come back to. And, it's why there must be recognition; adequate recognition—and honour and help, afforded them. Another thing it does is forge ties and bonds that are difficult for those who've not been there, to grasp. Deep. Brother carrying and encouraging brother, traversing together a massive thing over which they have no control; a thing larger, louder, more overwhelming, more demanding and immanent than anything ever conceived in their minds. We stand in both awe and in debt.

Norman turned out to be a gentleman of the old school. Of course, we made arrangements to meet—to visit him at his home in Asquith where he greeted us with great warmth and delight. And then, over the indispensable cup of tea, regaled my wife and me with story after story of those extraordinary days. Sometimes tea works even better than beer.

★ ★ ★

CHAPTER 10

MAX BARRINGTON

Edward Tench had tried his hand at many things, but among his first loves was photography. He had a studio in Auburn, a suburb of Sydney. Only a few of his photographs remain. However, there was one that I could not have known about that was soon to come to light.

"Is there a Max Barrington on this number?"

"Yes" responded the woman at the other end, "who is calling?"

"My name is Ian Heard and I think my father was with Max in the war—and if I may, I'd like to speak with him."

"Just a moment, I'll get him for you."

"Thank you."

"Hullo?"

"Hullo Max; are you the Max Barrington who served with 7th Division Provost in World War Two?"

"Yes, I am."

"Does the name Edward or Teddy Tench mean anything to you, Max?" Again, something of a lump in my throat, not knowing what to expect; what I might hear that perhaps I did not want to hear.

"Teddy? The mad photographer?" (Remember, more than 60 years have passed!)

"Well, yes; how did you know he was a photographer?" Pulse quickening now; mysterious sense of connection and fulfillment again with the pulse.

"Ah…he brought his Rolleiflex camera with him when we boarded the Queen Mary out of Sydney. Teddy used to take pictures of the boys on the way to Egypt. Who are you?"

"Max, I'm Teddy's son."

"Well, I'll be blowed. Where is he? Is Ted still alive?"

"No, he died in the New Guinea campaign."

"Yeah, I thought I heard that."

"Max, may I come and meet with you for a chat?"

"Of course… be good to meet you."

And so, arrangements were made and I once again marvelled at the memory and the never-forgotten camaraderie of men who've stood shoulder to shoulder in the ugliest thing that life on earth can throw at them. No wonder they love to get together on ANZAC Day. It reminds; it affirms; and it is good. But it is better when they see the fruit of their courageous action in well-bred and respectful generations who have not forgotten. That's why it is good to see some of today's generation visiting the battlegrounds on which the freedoms they might otherwise so easily take for granted, were won.

The only visit I had with Max was also wonderful where, of course, over the ubiquitous and indispensable cup of tea and a bickie … "Your father loved to help everyone… used to take photos of the boys and send them home to their missus's and families from various ports and when we reached the Middle East."

"Really, but…" I was about to ask how he processed them when Max told me that not only did he bring his beloved camera; he also brought lots of film and processing chemicals in his luggage!

Max laughed, "there was a time or two when the blokes got a bit cranky with him."

"Oh?"

"Yeah, they couldn't use the bath in our part of the ship because your father had made it a temporary dark-room and was developing pictures in the tub!" Much laughter ensued as, like the pictures emerging from the bath-tub, the picture of my father was developing before my eyes!

More stories followed, of his popularity and honesty and goodness— and I could tell it was not in any way contrived for my benefit. It was coming from Max's heart. My heart swelled. Tears did too, on more than one occasion.

"Max, I don't suppose there's any chance you happen to have one of those photos." A moment or two's thought …

"As a matter of fact—yes—now I think about, would you believe, I do" as Max went off to another room and sounds of rummaging could be heard, I waited, not patiently—effecting small talk with Max's 'missus', whilst a lump in my throat made its presence felt!

Max emerged with an old photograph, monochrome of course, of the prow of the Queen Mary at anchor in Sydney Harbour, as he said,

"He took this as we were being taken out on a lighter to go aboard her in Sydney. You can keep it; it means something to me but it means a lot more to you." What a gesture! Hard to express gratitude for that.

There was another, too, in Gregory McCormack who also remembered my father, but with no definition to add. He certainly remembered him across those years, but had had little contact with him in the Provost Service—just remembered him as a likeable man. Nevertheless, he was glad to hear from me.

I told you that I had a sense that I was not organising this. It was being organised for me.

★ ★ ★

CHAPTER 11

NORMAN MAKES A HIT!

In those times I was having a regular breakfast with a group of pastors from various churches along the Northern Beaches region of Sydney. It was soon after meeting Norman McFarland and one morning I was telling them the story to date. They all enjoyed it immensely and one, Alan, said, "Ian, you just must come and share your story with the men of our church…they will love it."

We agreed and a date for a Saturday morning breakfast was set. Alan's was a fairly large congregation with a new building and excellent facilities in a beautiful bushland setting.

As the date drew near, I was looking forward to the opportunity. Out of the blue, just two days before the event, I was prompted to call Norman to see if he could accompany me to the breakfast. How delighted I was when he jumped at the opportunity even though it meant that I had to be up at 5.30 am to travel some distance away from our breakfast venue, I knew it would be worthwhile.

On arrival, I simply introduced Norman to the hosts and those sharing our table, as a friend whom I had brought along for the morning—but the surprise was to come! After our meal, I was introduced and launched into my story to a rapt audience, many of whom, of course, were men whose fathers or uncles or family members had also served in World War ll.

When I arrived at the part in the narrative reflecting on my tentative call to Norman McFarland and what a joy it had been to discover someone who remembered so well my father, I was then able to say, "and gentlemen, I have a wonderful surprise for you this morning. It is my very great pleasure to be able to introduce to you…Norman McFarland!"

Well, to say there was an eruption is an understatement! All had been so engaged and immersed in my story that to see the dear man of whom I spoke, with them in the here and now resulted in an outburst of spontaneous applause and admiration. What a delight it was to have Norman stand and acknowledge them and then for a few minutes add validity and colour to the story of the evacuation from Greece and of my father, following which he received more applause! I could tell he was both ignited and delighted by the recognition and appreciation.

Needless to say, Norman became a firm friend and we were able to share many enjoyable times together before his death on 28th May 2008.

On one occasion we visited the Military Police Museum at the Holsworthy Barracks on the outskirts of Sydney's south west. There too, he was feted and I was to discover that my father's name is engraved on a commemorative plaque on the parade ground.

★ ★ ★

CHAPTER 12

A PARABLE

I indicated that I believed that my story had a Superintendence upon it. I had seen too many 'coincidences' in its discovery to believe otherwise and here comes the part where I don't want to lose you. For I know that for some, when anyone begins to talk seriously about a Superintendent with a capital 'S' the temperature (for no actually logical reason) may suddenly drop a few degrees—and there are those who may be inclined to say (in both heart and mind) "oh no." But stay with me. Hear me out as I walk with you through what is a beautiful simile.

Because I am a Christian believer it was not difficult for me to see some very clear parallels in my journey of discovery to find and to 'know' my father—with the journey taken by many to discover their Heavenly Father.

That I had a father, of course I knew. A real father—the one from whom my DNA and life derived and to whom I owed my existence. Yet he seemed remote and unknowable; untouchable. And in a sense, mythical. There were certain evidences in some touchable items; medals, a dog-tag, papers, stories—but, they were not he. They did, however, point strongly to him and aroused desire. I was separated from him by what seemed, from where I stood, an unbridgeable gap.

We know we have a Father

Similarly, every one of us at some time senses that our deepest being, our very deepest reality, really has an Origin beyond mere humanity. And, at those moments there arises a longing for connection—actually, re-connection. Unless we are taught or informed, the yearning at one's deepest level and in our quietest, most private moments—the quest to know the 'I am' that is most deeply me, to answer the 'who am I' question—is not recognised for what it truly is. For I believe that we are not complete, do not arrive at full 'who-ness' until we know The Father from whom we derive, and have a restored relationship with Him. Meantime, we longingly sense that we have such a Father with a capital 'F' to whom we owe our existence at its core. We may manage temporarily to silence the longing by filling life up with a million things we think—or are told—will bring us 'home', but these things eventually prove unable. For physical things or events or people can never be the answer to the need that lies at the core of our being.

And so—to many *He* seems distant, mythical, probably unknowable. Certainly beyond the possibility of encounter, whilst at the same time, deep within the heart of many remains the yearning to find its own true Origin, its Father. Because of the 'noise' we often generate in what we don't even realise is a search, we may not recognise it for what it actually is. Yet there it is, in our alone-est moments…a gnawing hollowness we want to fill—and a sense of an empty space where something…a just-out-of-reach something, ought to be; a yearned-for thing that will deliver me safe home to peaceful certitude about the 'who' of ME—and indeed, the purpose of me.

This helps explain the enormous demand for, and popularity of, ancestry research. But no amount of that, as good as it may be, will connect with the Father who actually awaits our discovery of Him.

Many have become inured to such deep-in longing; have become dismissive of it, or simply suppress it beneath further layers of activity or entertainments or busy-ness that steal away opportunity for quietness of heart.

But we know we have a Father. His imprint is in our being—as is His beckoning call to us.

There is a Record

Returning to my journey, the next discovery I made was that a record existed and was accessible, in which I could discover my father's deeds and exploits! I had not known of the existence of such records, or, if I had read of war diaries, had no idea that they contained such rich and extraordinary information. Now, having been pointed to them, I made remarkable discoveries about my father. As we turned those long-ago pages, there, being disclosed to me, was my father and what he had done in behalf of so many. I was surprised at what was there...as I've indicated, from the sublime to the humorous! But all certainly, real.

As I've written, the discovery was filled with awe and wonder. My father was taking at least some form before my eyes—becoming a true and real person. The shadow was becoming substance as I began to discover and indeed, in a profound sense, know, my father! The deeds and exploits of a person, and how they are carried out, define a person; make them real. I saw a man who volunteered, was disciplined and courageous and selfless; who lived up to the mission and the motto of his calling and I felt that I began to understand...and know him.

This record had been there all along, accessible at any time during all those years of my ignorance of its real treasure. My ignorance of the record made no difference to its truth, it just remained veiled to me until I received some prompting, searched—and found. There are a thousand human accounts of war events, but actuality is found in the War Diaries because they were set down by those who were commissioned to do so; right there, experiencing the immediacy of what occurred—and under authority to record it accurately. They were not open to embellishment— witnesses and chains of command ensured truthfulness and accuracy.

Our heavenly Father's 'diary' is freely available to enable us to be brought near and to know Him. As with the War Diaries, the record is deliberate and has been set down under His superintending hand so that truth about Him and about what has been accomplished in our behalf, can be known. Many however, are ignorant of its existence and of what it reveals, but— He is there! His deeds and exploits on our behalf, why He did what He did; the story from beginning to end, cohesive, under-standable, making Him, real! Within those pages, He can be touched and connection can begin, yes, with the very One we actually most long to meet. In them He is disclosed as being for us, caring about us and with every action being with the intention of bringing us to Himself. Investigation brings great reward, as that record itself says, 'The unfold-ing of your words gives light; it gives understanding to the simple.'[6]

The experience of others

Beyond those pages however, something more awaited. For not only had I discovered my father in the record, but now I met others who actually knew him and had experience of his presence in their lives! They bore

---

[6]   Psalm 119:130 NIV

personal testimony to knowing and experiencing my father! They spoke of my father as a reality in their lives and what a thrill it was to hear their testimony. What I had read in the record was validated perfectly by what these witnesses to its truth, told me! There was a beautiful congruence which quickly made my father even more real and admirable.

It is this author's unshakeable conviction that in the journey of discovery that the one known as Heavenly Father takes people on, toward Him, not only does He bring them to His record: He usually also introduces them to people who know Him and bear testimony of that personal knowledge and relationship with Him. It is part of the journey to Him. We can believe or we can ignore such testimony, but to ignore or refuse to receive its truth will leave us impoverished and at distance from our true Father.

There is a Call and a Superintendence

In my case, once I began to respond to the enquiry that lay deep in my heart, things began to occur and to fall into place that were not of my doing or organisation. On a whim, I 'found' the photographs on the AWM website. They excited and gave impetus. I 'found' the story of *'The men who saved Australia'* and was moved to connect with Professor David Horner. He continued to point the way so that I 'found' the War Diaries and 'found' the book which 'just happened' to include my father. I 'found' the author, Glenn Wahlert and through him, just before too late, 'found' men who had been intimately connected with E A Tench!

When anyone begins to enquire of that thirst which is deepest within—honestly to seek true Origin—and does so with recognition that it is a Person they seek (not a vague force or philosophy)—it is my belief that there will be a Superintendence by that One upon their quest.

We are here on Purpose

Of course, if anyone has a reason to believe this, it is I. No, not chance or random, haphazard happenstance. Whilst the world appears the be random and chaotic, the chaos is in fact artfully and wonderfully, ordered. Quantum physicists are discovering the principal of chance and probability are at the core of matter. Yet, back of the apparent chaos is ultimate order. We just cannot get far enough back to see it—and that is exactly why we are called to trust Another! For the order appears as we retreat—like a large canvas which we cannot understand up close. But as we move back, and back even further, the picture emerges and we see the landscape and the picture makes more sense. And that is why God has given us via His word, a sky view. The street-level view is awful. It makes little sense, but the view from above reveals a great plan—and a destination. Yes, every one of us is here on purpose—and the first step in finding our part in The Purpose begins with our first move toward our Father in heaven!

It is the home-coming He awaits, just like the father in Jesus' famous story of the Prodigal Son who came home.[7]

---

[7] See Luke 15:11-32

★ ★ ★

CHAPTER 13

NORMAN ARRIVES 'HOME'

My adventure with Norman was exciting; for both of us. He had enjoyed immensely his shining moment and the appreciation afforded him at the men's breakfast. And we continued to be firm friends until he died in 2008. We journeyed together to spend a day at the Provost Museum at the Holsworthy Military Base on Sydney's south-western outskirts and we lunched together on several occasions. But I must tell you of the outcome of the breakfast...

As I concluded my presentation that morning, I encouraged any present who had not 'come home' to their Heavenly Father, to seek Him, and to do so now. He awaits our response to His open invitation to be joined with Him again and to receive the Life He offers all who desire to be joined again to Him. I concluded with a prayer, asking that any who desired to establish, or re-establish that Father-son relationship with Him to silently join me. The prayer went something like this—

"Father in heaven, we thank you for your grace. We thank you that you created us like you and to be in relationship with you as sons and daughters. We thank you for all you've done to restore that damaged relationship; for you have done everything necessary through your Son, Jesus Christ with whom we can join in knowing you as Father. I ask for, and receive, the forgiveness you offer through Him for my behaviour as a rebellious son and for rejecting you as Father. I pray for your life within me now to enable me to live as your son, re-joined to you, amen."

Following were several conversations and shortly Norman and I packed up my mementos and headed home. We had not gone far when Norman asked me, "Ian, you know that prayer you prayed at the close this morning…I wonder if you'd be so kind as to write that out for me?"

I said, "Of course, Norman, I'd be glad to. Is that because you wish to use it?" To which he replied,

"Ian, yes I do want to. But I want to do more than that. I want to take it with me to my dear wife's graveside and read it and say it there."

I hoped the lump I felt in my throat was not visible! This dear man, once a church-goer and perhaps close to being a true follower of Jesus, now wished to seal his relationship with his eternal Father—and to make it as concrete and inviolable as he felt he could by doing so beside the remains of his beloved of many years! And he confirmed with me later that he had done just that. What a sweet, sweet joy. Norman had come home to his wonderful, loving Father above!

My search has taken me on a fascinating journey of disclosure and I have been afforded opportunity to share it with many people in churches, in service clubs, in Israel to a tour group and even on a ship at sea. My wife and I had taken a small ship expedition cruise from Jakarta, Indonesia just a few years ago. The trip included the Spice Islands and up to the north of Papua and New Guinea. We disembarked in Madang and were flown south to conclude the trip in Port Moresby where our itinerary included a day's outing to Ower's Corner, the start of the Kokoda Track. On the return journey, we had a short time at the Bomana War Cemetery. When the tour operators learned of my story, I had been invited to share it on board and I'm thankful to report that it added a rich dimension to the visit to that cemetery. What had been seen by most as the last visit of a memorable trip, suddenly took on immense interest as all 84 guests were now very eager to visit grave No. B1.F. 15, that of E A Tench MM. And to cap the visit, the tour operators had organised both a floral tribute and a small youth choir from a local church to sing a hymn or two at the graveside. Hardly a dry eye among us!

I have been thankful for both the journey and its destination. It reminded me—in a time when many place unwarranted value on things of little worth—just how many heroes went to defend a cause they considered worth dying for. Medals of such recognition as my father's may be rare, but that does not mean heroes are rare. In most cases, every one of them deserved recognition and honour. It is gratifying to me that so many young Australians are, in our day, paying tribute to those who have laid down their lives in both great wars as well as the others we have been involved in. They are walking Kokoda; they are making pilgrimage to Gallipoli and the Somme and Beer Sheva; they are visiting the killing fields to pay their respects—and they will never be the same. It is not possible to stand in those places and in those cemeteries, to walk among the young dead, without arriving at a deep reverence—and a sense of gratitude.

Many on such pilgrimages are paying honour and respect. To fathers and perhaps mothers, to grandparents or uncles. Some are seeking a sense of identity and connection and place—even purpose. Some are seeking information and some are altruistic, hoping to prevent recurrences of the past tragedies—and travesties. But all—and each—have this one thing in common. They each have a loving and wonderful Heavenly Father, who can be sought, and found; and who desires to be found.

He said, "you shall seek for me and you *shall find me* when you search for me with all your heart."[8]

It is, above all searches, *the* search worth taking!

---

[8] Jeremiah 29:13

Australian 🛡 Military Forces

TELEPHONE

Please quote this Number when Replying

| 99817 |

Address
Records Office,
N.S.W.L. of C. Area,
R.A.S. Showground,
SYDNEY.

13 SEP 1945

AWARD OF THE MILITARY MEDAL.

NX 14771 Cpl. E. A. TENCH.

CITATION.

"On the morning of the 18th of April '41, Col. Rogers of 1 Aust. Corps, sought from this Coy. information regarding the whereabouts of the 21st Batt. N.Z. Forces. This intelligence was of the utmost importance, because the safety of the "LEE Forces" who were in defensive position near DOMOKOS was linked with the withdrawal of the 21st Batt. along the VOLOS Rd. to MOLOS. Cpl. Tench volunteered to undertake the journey from near BRALLOS PASS to MOLOS, to N.Z. Brigade H.Q. and thence to H.Q. "LEE Forces" DOMOKOS. Cpl. Tench left with a despatch from Col. Rogers at 0730 hrs., and returned at 1530 hrs., with his task accomplished. During this period the road along which Cpl. Tench motor cycled was continuously bombed and machine gunned. There is no doubt that the courage and devotion to duty shown by Cpl. Tench in getting the despatch through without thought for his own personal safety assisted not a little to the successful withdrawal of the "LEE Force".

* * *

Military Medal Description

Created in 1916 by King George V for other ranks in the Army to correspond with the Military Cross instituted two years earlier, but eventually back dated in availability to 1914. Awarded to other ranks for 'acts of gallantry and devotion to duty under fire'.

Discontinued in 1993 when the Military Cross was made available to all ranks. The ribbon is principally of dark blue with three white and two crimson vertical stripes in the cental third. Australians have won a very large number of Medals in the campaigns to 1972 when the last award to an Australian was made. 11,038 Military Medals were awarded to Army personnel and 14 to Air Force members. 478 first Bars were awarded, 15 second Bars and a unique third Bar to a stretcher bearer with the 55th Infantry Battalion AIF in World War 1, Private E A Corey, meaning he had won the Medal four times.

From http://www.itsanhonour.gov.au/honours/awards/imperial.cfm#mc

Bombs bursting on the Lamia-Domokos Road along which E A Tench had to motorcycle (Picture courtesy Australian War Memorial)

Above: Captain J Grimshaw, Warrant Officer I F Harris and Staff Sergeant E A Tench astride their Norton Motorcycles in Aley, Lebanon (Picture courtesy Australian War Memorial).

Below: Trucks and vehicles of Allied Forces retreating through Brallos Pass (Picture courtesy Australian War Memorial)

Above: A Provost rides ahead of a convoy through the bombed out town of Larisa (Picture courtesy Australian War Memorial).

Below: Bombed trucks near Domokos (Picture courtesy Australian War Memorial)

Above: 2/9 General Field Hospital near Hombrom's Bluff, 27 Kms from Port Moresby (Picture courtesy Australian War Memorial).

Below: HM Troopship Queen Mary at anchor in Sydney Harbour 1940

Norman McFarland on an ANZAC Day march.

Military Medal * 1939 - 45 Star * Africa Star * Pacific Star * Defence Medal * War Medal * Australian Service Medal * Greece

Military Medal (MM)

The MM was instituted in March 1916 as an award for non-officer rank of the Army for acts of bravery. In the First World War the MM was awarded to a few recipients from the Royal Navy and Royal Air Force. Some RAF personnel were awarded the MM during World War II. All MMs are issued named with the recipient's details impressed around the medal's rim.

During World War I, 115,000 MMs were awarded, with 5,800 first bars and 180 second bars. There

Opposite page top: E A Tench's Medals including Military Medal at far left.

Opposite page below: The Miltary Medal: For Bravery in the Field.

This page top right: Citation for E A Tench's Military Medal.

This page below right: Lieutenant Edward Alfred Tench in uniform with Military Medal Colour Bar over heart.

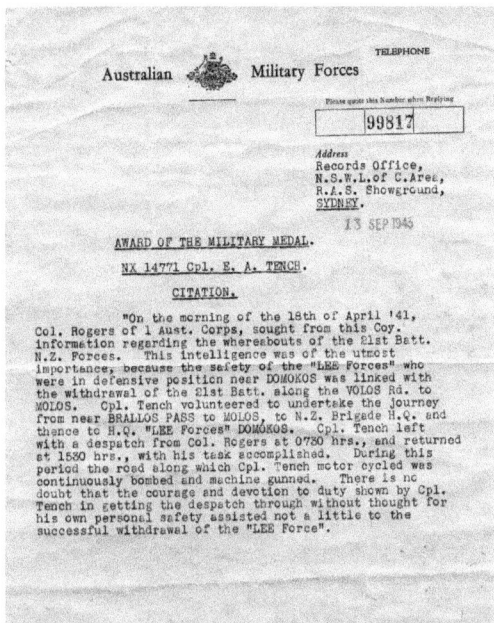

Australian Military Forces

TELEPHONE

Please quote this Number when Replying

99817

Address
Records Office,
N.S.W.L.of C.Area,
R.A.S. Showground,
SYDNEY.

13 SEP 1945

AWARD OF THE MILITARY MEDAL.

NX 14771 Cpl. E. A. TENCH.

CITATION.

"On the morning of the 18th of April '41, Col. Rogers of 1 Aust. Corps, sought from this Coy. information regarding the whereabouts of the 21st Batt. N.Z. Forces. This intelligence was of the utmost importance, because the safety of the "LEE Forces" who were in defensive position near DOMOKOS was linked with the withdrawal of the 21st Batt. along the VOLOS Rd. to MOLOS. Cpl. Tench volunteered to undertake the journey from near BRALLOS PASS to MOLOS, to N.Z. Brigade H.Q. and thence to H.Q. "LEE Forces" DOMOKOS. Cpl. Tench left with a despatch from Col. Rogers at 0730 hrs., and returned at 1530 hrs., with his task accomplished. During this period the road along which Cpl. Tench motor cycled was continuously bombed and machine gunned. There is no doubt that the courage and devotion to duty shown by Cpl. Tench in getting the despatch through without thought for his own personal safety assisted not a little to the successful withdrawal of the "LEE Force".

was 1 award of the MM and 3 bars. World War II saw the award of 15,000 MMs (total for all Commonwealth countries) with 164 first bars and 2 second bars.

Although all MMs awarded are listed in the London Gazette, the First World War MMs don't have citations. The Second World War MMs generally do have citations.

Following the 1993 review this medal has been replaced by the Military Cross, which is now available to all ranks.

Left: Grave of E A Tench
MM. Grave No. B1.F.15;

Below: Bomana War
Cemetery near Port
Moresby PNG.

www.ingramcontent.com/pod-product-compliance
Lightning Source LLC
LaVergne TN
LVHW051607080426
835510LV00020B/3167